Magic piano book

for 4 year olds

Primer Level A

For the young beginner

Lucia Timková

Copyright © 2013 Lucia Timková

All rights reserved.

ISBN-13: 978-1490375946
ISBN-10: 1490375945

Teachers and Parents

This method provides solid training for beginners, from the youngest to the oldest, using easy ways to make quick progress without difficulties in understanding. To help with the teaching process, many coloured pictures and graphics use the student's visual memory to get a strong and secure grasp of the basics uses.

- Students gain an understanding of the basic important theory using many coloured pictures to prompt their visual memory to help them understand and use it in their exercises in practice songs and to practice/test it in the workbook.

- Note-reading skills. The students are to say the names of the notes aloud and count them while they play the exercises on the piano. This makes students realize what notes they are playing, which is not easy. They don't learn it by memorising using the finger guide or by memorising the melody. Rather, they have to know the exact note names. They read notes from the very start.

- Each finger or a new note is individually and strongly developed using a lot of exercises for particular subjects from the beginning with a graduated, consistent method.

- Another strength is the introduction of ensemble playing from the very beginning. Beginner students have to play each exercise three times: say letter names while they play, count while they play, and play with a teacher. This is important for the teacher to help guide the student and to make sure that students understand the individual notes and already know how to play each exercise before they go home. When the students can read music, performing becomes a joy rather than a dreaded experience.

- In the workbook, which is included for each level you are going to confirm the notes and the theory/terminology you have learned during the lesson in three steps, which should be done in each lesson. Writing the notes, finding the notes on the staff/stave in different orders and playing the game "Noughts and Crosses" where students are drawing and explaining the symbols to help them remember it.

- After students have completed books A/B for four year olds, 1A/1B and 2A/2B, they are competent in music terminology and sight reading. They have a solid enough understanding to begin studying books of other composers; Classical or Christmas books at that particular level.

Magic Piano book 1A begins by reviewing the same concepts taught in Magic Piano A/B for four year olds and also introduces new concepts for the left hand, with progression to book 1B.

CONTENTS

The piano keyboard – two/ three back keys …………............................…...….….…………….	2
All C's ……………………………………………………………………………………….…...	3
Fingering – Each finger has a number – right hand ……………………………….……………..	4
Fingering – Each finger has a number – left hand ……………………………….……………...	5
Stave/ Staff ………………………………………………………………………….………….	6
Treble clef …………………………….....……………………………………….…………..	7
Bar lines/ Bar/ Double line ……………………………………………………….…….…..……	8
Time Signature ………………......……………………………………………………...…………..	9
Whole note/ Semibreve C – clapping …………………………………………….........…………	10
Review – Whole note/ Semibreve C in the Treble ………………………………………..……....	11
Half note/ Minim C – clapping ……………………………………………………….....………..	12
Review – Half note/ Minim C ……………………………………………...…..……....…………...	13
Quarter note/ Crotchet C – clapping …………………………………………….…..…..………….	14
Review – Quarter note/ Crotchet C …………………………………………………….…………...	15
Dynamics – Forte/ Piano ……………………………………………………….………………..	16
Review – We are going to school …....……..…..………………………………….………………..	17
Review – Hi, hi crocodile ……………………………………………………….....………………..	18
Review – Teddy bear ………………………………………………………..…….………………..	19

Review – Cow	20
Review – One, two, three	21
Review – Mice	22
New note – D in the Treble	23
Review – Breakfast	24
Legato/ Staccato	25
Review – Butterfly	26
Review – Ladybird	27
Review – Rainbow	28
Review – Playground	29
New note – E in the Treble	30
Crescendo and Decrescendo	31
Review – Frog	32
Review – Monkeys	33
Review – Mary had a little lamb	34
Review – Magic word please	35
Dotted half note/ Dotted minim	36
Review – Ballet – dancer	37
Review – Flowers	38
Review – Train	39
Certificate	40

This book belongs to:

_____

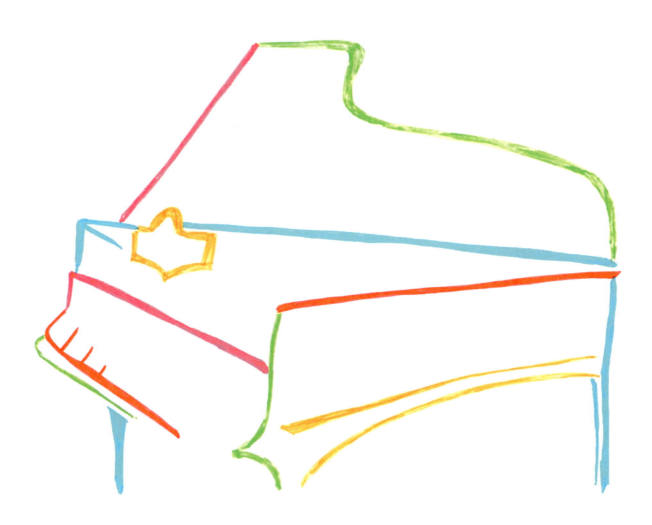

The piano keyboard has white and black keys.
The Black keys are in groups of 2's and 3's.

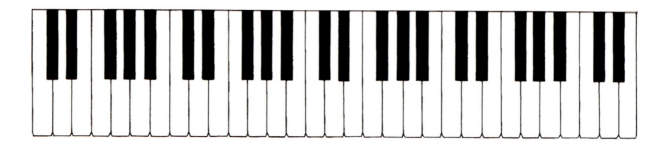

1) Touch all the groups of two black keys.
2) Touch all the groups of three black keys.

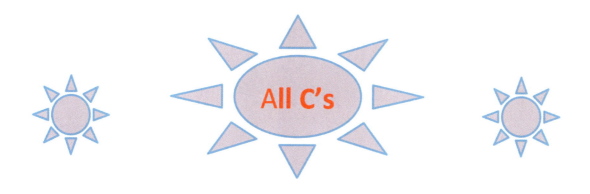

C is found to the left of the TWO BLACK KEYS.

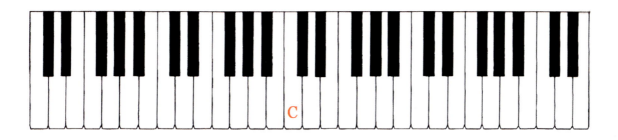

Middle C

Touch all the groups of TWO black keys.
Touch all the groups of THREE black keys.
Play all the C's on the piano.

Each finger has a number

1) Point to your 1st, 2nd, 3rd, 4th, 5th finger.
2) Play and count to 4.
3) Play with your teacher.

The thumbs are both numbered

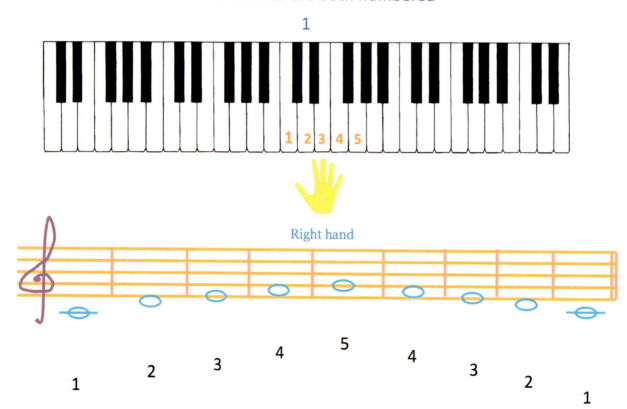

Accompaniment - Student plays one octave higher

1) Point to your 1st, 2nd, 3rd, 4th, 5th finger.
2) Play and count to 4.
3) Play with your teacher.

Each finger has a number

The thumbs are both numbered

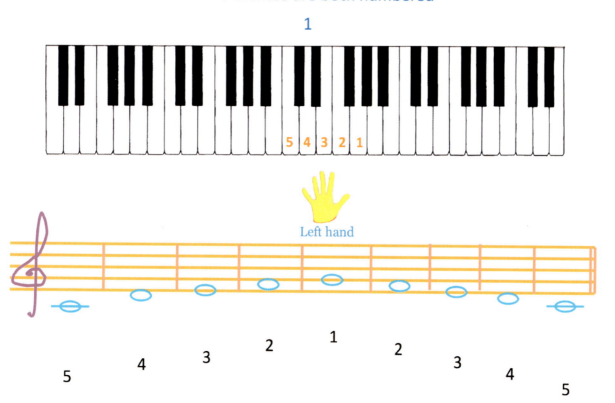

Accompaniment - Student plays one octave higher

Stave, Staff

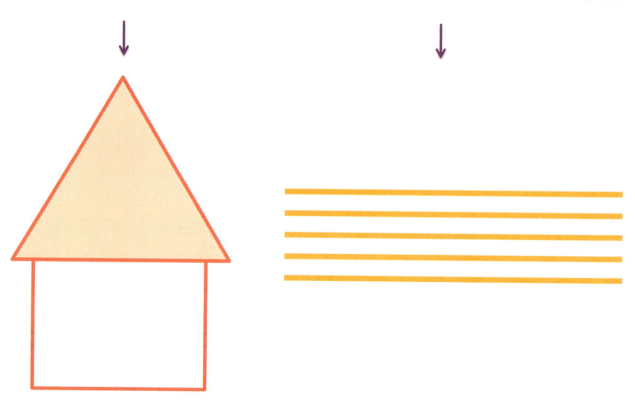

People live in a house. The notes live in the house called a stave or staff.

It has 5 lines with spaces in between.

Treble Clef play with your right hand

What do we need
if we want to open the house?

If we want to start playing the music we
also need a key – called **treble clef.**

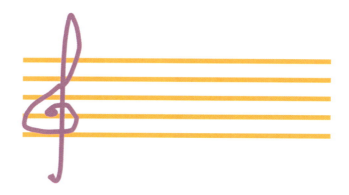

Bar lines/ Bar- Measure

In a house we have walls. In music we have walls called ' bar lines '. The space between the walls in a house is a room. The space between the bar lines is called a bar / measure. At the end of the song is the double bar-line and it tells you that song has finished.

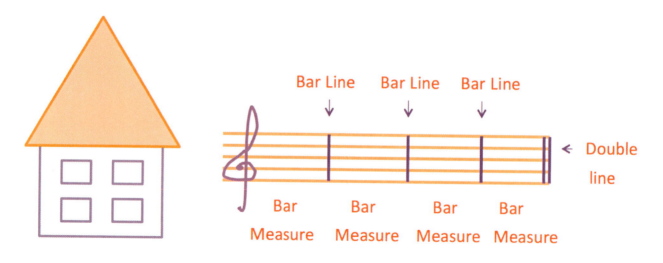

1) How many BAR LINES can you see?
2) How many rooms can you see in the house?
3) How many bars can you see in the stave?
4) Where is the double bar line?

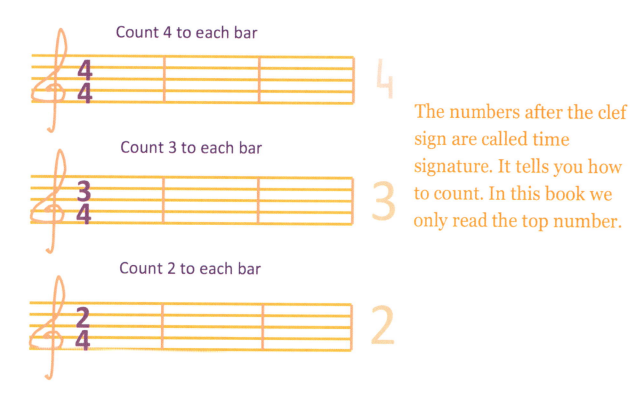

The numbers after the clef sign are called time signature. It tells you how to count. In this book we only read the top number.

1) What does top number 4 mean?
2) What does top number 3 mean?
3) What does top number 2 mean?
4) What do we call the numbers?

Whole note - Semibreve = 4 beats

This is a musical note called a whole note sometimes a semibreve. It lasts for four counts.

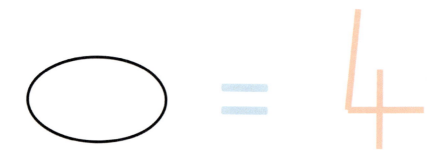

1) Clap the rhythm and count four to each note.

Whole note C
Semibreve

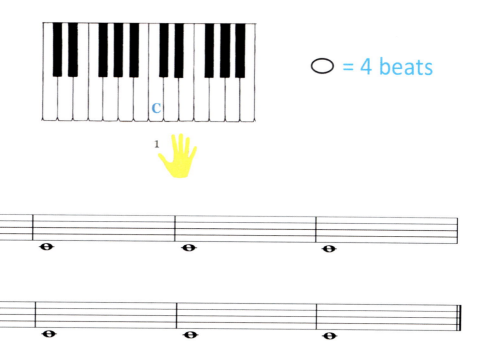

$\circ$ = 4 beats

1) Play and say the letter names of the notes.
2) Play and count till four.
3) Play with your teacher and listen to the song.

Accompaniment

Half note C
Minim

This is a musical note called a half note sometimes minim. It lasts for two counts.

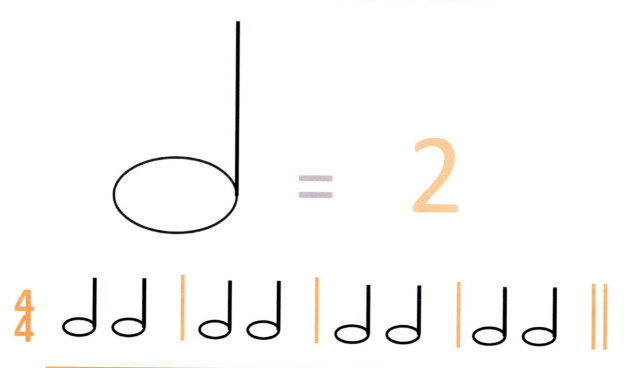

1) Clap the rhythm and count one-two to the first note and three-four to the second note of each bar.

Half note C
Minim

𝅗𝅥 = 2 beats

One-two   three-four

1) Play and say the letter names of the notes.
2) Play with your right hand and count one-two to the first note and three-four to the second note of each bar.
3) Play with your teacher and listen to the song.

Accompaniment

Quarter Note C
Crotchet

This is a musical note called a quarter note sometimes crotchet. It lasts for one count.

♩ = 1

4/4 ♩♩♩♩ | ♩♩♩♩ | ♩♩♩♩ ||

1) Clap the rhythm and count till four.

Quarter Note C
Crotchet

♩ = 1 beat

One two three four

1) Play and say the letter names of the notes.
2) Play and count till four.
3) Play with your teacher and listen to the song.

Accompaniment

Dynamics - loud and soft

f = forte = loud   **p** = piano = soft

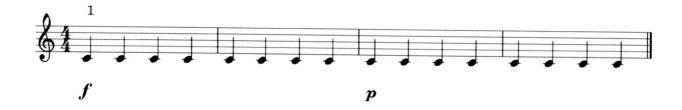

1) Play and say the letter names of the notes.
2) Play and count till four.
3) Play with dynamics.

Accompaniment

We are going to school

> 1) Play and say the letter names of the notes.
> 2) Play and count till four.
> 3) Play and sing the song.

Hi, hi, crocodile

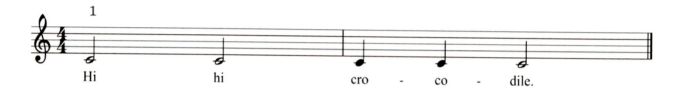

Hi   hi   cro - co - dile.

1) Play and say the letter names of the notes.
2) Play and count till four.
3) Play and sing the song.

Teddy bear

Te - ddy   bear   te - ddy   bear   stay   with   me   eve - ry   day.

1) Play and say the letter names of the notes.
2) Play and count till four.
3) Play and sing the song.

Cow

The top number 2 means count each bar till 2.

1) Play and say the letter names of the notes.
2) Play and count till two.
3) Play and sing the song.

One, two, three

The top number 3 means count each bar till 3.

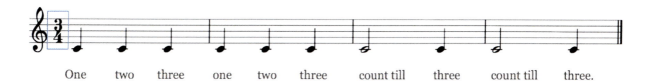

One two three one two three count till three count till three.

1) Play and say the letter names of the notes.
2) Play and count till three.
3) Play and sing the song.

Mice

The top number 4 means count each bar till 4.

1) Play and say the letter names of the notes.
2) Play and count till four.
3) Play and sing the song.

New note

D

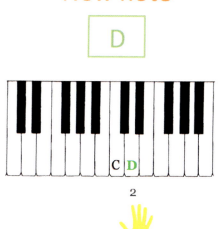

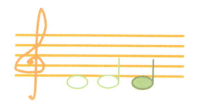

1) Play and say the letter names of the notes.
2) Play and count till four.
3) Play and listen to the song.

Breakfast

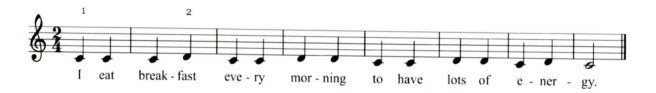

1) Play and say the letter names of the notes.
2) Play and count till two.
3) Play and sing the song.

Legato

Legato means to play the notes smoothly.
So they are connected to each other.

Staccato

A dot over or under the head of the
note makes it short and detached.

1) Play and say the letter names of the notes.
2) Play and count till two.
3) Play legato - staccato.

Butterfly

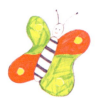

1) Play and say the letter names of the notes.
2) Play and count till four.
3) Play with your teacher and sing the song.

Accompaniment

Ladybird

1) Play and say the letter names of the notes.
2) Play and count till four.
3) Play with your teacher and sing the song.

Accompaniment

Rainbow

1) Play and say the letter names of the notes.
2) Play and count till four.
3) Play with your teacher and sing the song.

Accompaniment

Playground

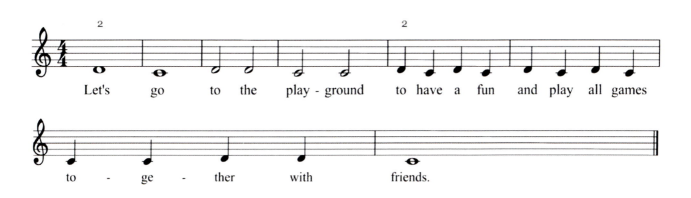

1) Play and say the letter names of the notes.
2) Play and count till four.
3) Play with your teacher and sing the song.

Accompaniment

New note
E

1) Play and say the letter names of the notes.
2) Play and count till four.
3) Play and listen to the song.

Crescendo
getting louder

Decrescendo
getting softer

1) Play and say the letter names of the notes.
2) Play and count till two.
3) Play with dynamics crescendo and decrescendo.

Frog

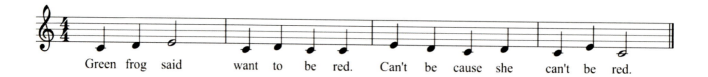

Green frog said want to be red. Can't be cause she can't be red.

1) Play and say the letter names of the notes.
2) Play and count till four.
3) Play with your teacher and sing the song.

Accompaniment

Monkeys

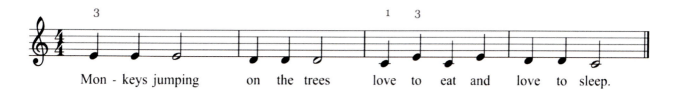

1) Play and say the letter names of the notes.
2) Play and count till four.
3) Play with your teacher and sing the song.

Accompaniment

Mary Had a Little Lamb

Accompaniment

1) Play and say the letter names of the notes.
2) Play and count till four.
3) Play wtih your teacher and sing the song.

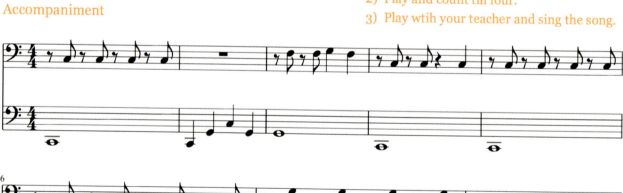

Magic word please

When you know a ma-gic word then you say please and it works.

1) Play and say the letter names of the notes.
2) Play and count till two.
3) Play and sing the song.

Dotted Half –note
The dotted minim

Looks like this

And is held for 3 counts.
A dot after a note increases its length by half (2+1=3).

Ballet-dancer

1) Play and say the letter names of the notes.
2) Play and count till three.
3) Play with your teacher and listen to the song.

Accompaniment

Flowers

Flo - wers flo - wers al - ways smell nice.

1) Play and say the letter names of the notes.
2) Play and count till three.
3) Play wtih your teacher and sing the song.

Accompaniment

Train

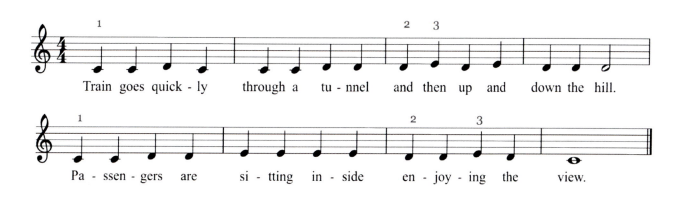

1) Play and say the letter names of the notes.
2) Play and count till four.
3) Play wtih your teacher and sing the song.

Accompaniment

Certificate

This is to certify that

_____

successfully completed

Magic piano book A

_____

and is eligible for promotion to

Magic piano book B

Congratulations!

_____

Teacher's signature

This course is carefully leveled into the following books :

Magic piano book for 4 year olds - Primer Level A   ISBN-13: 978-1490375946
Magic piano book for 4 year olds - Primer Level B   ISBN-13: 978-1490997391
Magic work book for 4 year olds - Primer Level A-B   ISBN-13: 978-1490997780

Magic piano book - Level 1A - For Beginners   ISBN-13: 978-1499722758
Magic piano book - Level 1B - For Beginners   ISBN-13: 978-1499723243
Magic work book - Level 1A-1B - For Beginners   ISBN-13: 978-1499723816

Magic piano book - Level 2A   ISBN-13: 978-1490999050
Magic piano book - Level 2B   ISBN-13: 978-1490999111
Magic work book - Level 2A-2B   ISBN-13: 978-1490999159

Sinterklaasliedjes – Niveau 2   ISBN-13: 978-1499724202

Made in the USA
Las Vegas, NV
01 June 2021